WHAT DID
YOU SAY?

WHAT DID YOU SAY?

a guide to oral and written communication

STANLEY B. FELBER
ARTHUR KOCH

Milwaukee Area Technical College
Milwaukee, Wisconsin

PRENTICE-HALL, INC., Englewood Cliffs, New Jersey

Library of Congress Cataloging in Publication Data

FELBER, STANLEY B.   1932–
    What did you say?

    1. Communication.   I. Koch, Arthur, 1931–
joint author.   II. Title.
P90.F4   808   72-10485
ISBN 0-13-951855-X

© 1973 by Prentice-Hall, Inc.
Englewood Cliffs, New Jersey

Printed in the United States of America

10   9   8   7   6   5   4   3   2   1

PRENTICE-HALL INTERNATIONAL, INC., London
PRENTICE-HALL OF AUSTRALIA, PTY. LTD., Sydney
PRENTICE-HALL OF CANADA, LTD., Toronto
PRENTICE-HALL OF INDIA PRIVATE LIMITED, New Delhi
PRENTICE-HALL OF JAPAN, INC., Tokyo

The quote from William A. Nail on p. v is taken from
"What Did You Say?" *Vital Speeches*, XXXVIII, No. 23 (September 15, 1971), 726.

prologue

The role of the broadcaster, the communicator, the
advertising copy writer, the public relations man, the
public speaker, the guy who writes the business letter,
the guy who writes the love letter, the guy who writes
the letter home—is to get ideas and information across
simply, in an easy to understand and attractive way.
Elizabeth Barrett Browning, in one of her Sonnets from the
Portuguese, "How Do I Love Thee" said more in a very few
lines about love than many of us could say in our broken
prose if we filled up as many pages as are in a Sears
Roebuck catalog.
What it all boils down to is this: Anybody who has
anything to say in words or in pictures to be transmitted
from one mind to another—regardless of all the modern
electronic paraphernalia and hard work you go through to
reach that reader, viewer or listener—has to ask himself
the question "What did you say?" before he begins to transmit.
The only way we can be sure that our ideas achieve their objective
is to be clear about what we want to say and who we are trying to
reach. That means understanding the guy on the other end. . . .

William A. Nail

contents

4

audience analysis · 43

5

attention · 65

6

supporting your ideas · 78

7

effective sentence structure · 105

8

effective paragraphing · 121

9

speech evaluation · 133

10

speech delivery · 147

11

persuasion · 169

preface

With the multitude of textbooks already available to freshman English classes, any new manuscript must justify itself. The distinctive feature of *What Did You Say?* is that it combines both oral and written communication skills within an integrated framework. An ever-increasing number of career-oriented educational programs in our community colleges, vocational and technical institutes, and universities has occasioned the rapid growth of communication courses. These courses seek to provide occupationally-minded students with the language skills that will enable them to function with efficiency and perception in society. It is to this market that our book is aimed.

Chapter 1 lays the foundation for the units that follow. Subsequent chapters deal with the planning, preparation, and presentation stages of effective communication. Most of the fifteen chapters are fully integrated; however, because differences between writing and speaking exist, some are devoted exclusively to either writing or speaking. While there is a logical progression from the basics to the more sophisticated aspects of communication, each chapter represents a self-contained study unit; consequently, chapters may be rearranged without disrupting the over-all plan of the book.

We are indebted to our colleagues at MATC for reading portions of the manuscript and making many positive suggestions and to our students for field testing all of the exercises and speech and writing assignments. We are particularly grateful to our wives, Estelle and Betty, for their constructive criticism and, above all, their patience and understanding. Finally, we are indebted to our children for trying to understand why so many of our evenings and weekends were spent preparing this manuscript. The better world we all seek can only come about through improved communication. For our children and all children we hope these pages represent a step in that direction.

Stanley B. Felber
Arthur Koch

1
an overview

WHY STUDY COMMUNICATION?

If you are like most high school graduates, the prospect of another year or two of English far from excites you. You have formally studied our complex, at times illogical language since elementary school, and you have engaged in the process of communication all your lives. Now college. And more English!

English teachers often pride themselves on the importance of their discipline. "We are the largest department on campus and rightly so. All students, regardless of future educational and vocational objectives, need to learn to communicate more effectively. A good command of language skills can lead to a challenging, creative future. Inadequate mastery of the techniques of communication can only lessen the possibilities available to you."

In recent years, English teachers have found a powerful ally in industry. Employees are frequently sent to college at company expense in an effort to improve their communication skills. The following excerpt from an industrial publication addressed to technical students is typical of industry's concern with language skills:

To understand and be understood. A good education provides the tools for understanding. The first and most important of these tools is language for communication. It may surprise you that we've begun by putting the need to study English first rather than stressing science or mathematics. After all, our business is primarily concerned with science and the useful application of technological developments. Nevertheless, we are convinced that no matter what your career, a command of the English language is the most important skill you can acquire. Learning rules of grammar and acquiring the abilities to write effectively and to read accurately are vital. This background provides the skill to express yourself in speaking and writing and to extract maximum meaning from the spoken and written words of others.

This process is called communications. In today's world, and even more so in tomorrow's, the person who cannot communicate clearly labors under a tremendous handicap.

The young engineer, for example, might have his most brilliant idea rejected if he is unable to explain its significance to others. In addition, he will be unable to keep up with advances in his own field if he cannot get the facts from the flood of technical information available to him.

Think of any career you like: teacher, naval engineer, actor, salesman, auditor, lawyer, physician, news reporter. Is there one in which you won't have to communicate effectively with others in order to perform successfully?

A time to prepare. The best foundation for whatever career you eventually choose is a broad-based education that increases your understanding and appreciation of everything in life.

It is essential that you start "building in" this kind of background now, for there is no way that you can predict the exact requirements of life or what your interests will be in the future. In short, now is the time to prepare for an education rather than a job.

Obviously, most successful careers today call for special training—often long and intensive. Does this mean that you must commit yourself now to a specific plan of action? Not necessarily. How can you plan for a career that may not even exist today?

The answer is stay flexible. Don't cut yourself off from the future. Keep to the march of knowledge in general. Top careers will more and more demand people with specialized skills in combination with diversified backgrounds.

If there is one rule you can apply that will keep the door open to almost any future career, it is this: when you have a choice of courses, pick those which will help broaden your background—mathematics, language, physical sciences, literature, the social studies.

There's always the chance you'll want to switch your field of study in midstream. Why not? That's one and only one of the advantages of starting with a sound basic education and staying flexible.

Reprinted with the permission of General Electric Company.

You probably agree that the arguments of education and industry have validity, but somehow a continuance of the day-to-day struggle with "nouns and verbs and stupid things like that," as one student put it, leaves you a bit cold. Perhaps you feel that English cannot be as stimulating as a course in your area of specialization, but we don't want you to think of your communication study as just another English course.

The pages that follow will involve you in the practical aspects of written and oral communication. You will discover that in the performance of one of life's most important functions—communicating effectively with your fellow human beings—language can be one of the most exciting and demanding of studies.

A PHILOSOPHY OF COMMUNICATION

Traditionally, language study has been fragmented and compartmentalized, involving separate courses in grammar, composition, and literature. Reading and listening have recently emerged as highly specialized fields within the study of language. Most high schools and colleges offer reading workshops, reading and study skills programs, and courses in speed reading. The last named has become a lucrative enterprise for private educational concerns that capitalize on our inability to assimilate ever-increasing amounts of printed material with speed and comprehension. According to the *Harvard Business Review*, "The busy executive spends 80% of his time . . . listening to people . . . and still doesn't hear half of what is said." *Nation's Business* reports that most of us "really absorb only a scant 30%" of what we hear. Our increasing awareness of the importance of effective listening has resulted in some highly specialized listening courses, most of them programmed. The subject matter of this book—language and communication—has been subdivided into numerous highly specialized fields which are usually studied separately. For practical and philosophical reasons, we propose to treat the study of language as a single subject.

Our treatment of communication is primarily intended for you, the college student. Because most of your course work is directly related to your chosen field of specialization, the amount of time set aside for general education courses in your curriculum is necessarily limited. It is usually impractical to schedule separate courses in speech, composition, literature, grammar, reading, and listening. Although this book does not attempt to combine all these skills, it does effect a workable, realistic compromise by integrating written and oral communication.

Furthermore, and more important, we believe an integrated approach to be philosophically sound. The communication skills, despite various conflicts among them, have much in common. We propose to indicate both their similarities and differences throughout our study.

THE SKILLS OF COMMUNICATION

Expressive Skills

Speaking and writing are generally referred to as expressive skills; they provide the means whereby we express ourselves to others. Both skills are usually discussed under the same heading, because effective speaking and writing involve many similar problems, such as selecting a subject, communicating purposefully, relating material to a single, dominant idea, and organizing logically.

Obviously, there are also important differences. Writing is a relatively private affair between you and your reader, allowing ample time for revision and correction. When you are speaking publicly, however, all eyes are focused on you. A mistake cannot be readily erased. Speaking and writing employ different means to achieve emphasis and variety, but the primary purpose of both skills is the same: to get the message to your audience in an interesting way.

Receptive Skills

When we listen or read, we receive information through the spoken word or printed page. However, frequently we *hear*, but do not really *listen*. An entry in the American College Dictionary clarifies the distinction between these two terms:

Hear, Listen apply to the perception of sound. To hear is to have such perception by means of the auditory sense: *to hear distant bells*. To listen is to give attention in order to hear and understand the meaning of a sound or sounds: *to listen to what is being said, to listen for a well-known footstep.*

Similarly, sometimes we read words without understanding their meaning. Have you ever spent an hour or so reading an assigned chapter without having more than a vague notion of its contents? Perhaps you were distracted by interruptions or your own thoughts. Concentration is essential to both listening and reading, with the basic difference that if you cannot concentrate on what you are reading, you can always return to it at another time. You cannot, however, expect your instructor to repeat his lecture after class because your thoughts drifted during his presentation. Both skills involve breaking down a communication into main ideas and supporting details. Listening to your instructor's lecture is more demanding than listening to a friend relate a personal experience; reading Spenser's *The Fairie Queene* requires more concentration than reading a popular novel like *The Godfather.* However, all effective reading and listening share a common purpose: to receive messages clearly.

THE COMMUNICATIVE ACT

Communication results when a response occurs to a stimulus. For example:

Stimulus	*Response*
1. Strong winds and heavy rain	Baby cries
2. Strong winds and heavy rain	Man closes window

Our stimuli for the above examples, strong winds and heavy rain, are nonverbal. The baby is frightened by the nonverbal stimuli, and his response is an automatic one based on fear. In the second example, the man's response is motivated by other considerations, perhaps his desire to block out outside noise, or to protect his family and his belongings. Because he must decide among alternatives, the man's response involves reasoning. Thus, we see that a response to a nonverbal stimulus may or may not be automatic.

Let us consider another stimulus-response situation:

Stimulus	*Response*
3. Dog barks	Baby cries
4. Dog barks	Man feeds dog

Although once again our stimulus is the same, this time it is verbal. The baby's response to the stimulus is automatic, again based on fear. The fourth example illustrates a nonautomatic response—feeding—to a verbal stimulus. Thus far we have differentiated between two types of stimuli, nonverbal and verbal, either of which can result in automatic or nonautomatic responses.

The stimulus in a communicative act includes a sender and a message. Study the following analyses of stimuli previously referred to:

Stimulus	=	*Sender* + *Message*
1. Strong winds and heavy rain		Depending upon your philosophical and theological convictions, you may conclude that "nature" or a supreme being is the *sender*; the *message*, strong winds and heavy rain, is then transmitted to a receiver.
2. Barking dog		The dog is the *sender*, his bark is the *message*.

Before one can respond to a stimulus (sender and message), he must first receive the message. Therefore, the response in an act of communication implies a receiver. Initially we defined communication as a response to a stimulus, but our modified definition now includes a sender, a message, a receiver, and a response.

Sender	*Message*	*Receiver*	*Response*
1. "Nature"	Strong winds and heavy rain	Baby	Crying
2. "Nature"	Strong winds and heavy rain	Man	Closing window
3. Dog	Bark	Baby	Crying
4. Dog	Bark	Man	Feeding dog

When a breakdown in communication occurs, one or more of the four basic requirements have not been fulfilled. If you tell a friend you will meet him outside a building after your class, and he waits patiently in front while you wait near the side entrance, the message you sent to him was either incomplete or misunderstood. If your instructor must ask you to repeat your answer to his question in an audible voice, you, as a sender, have failed to establish meaningful contact. If you jump the gun at a traffic light because you were thinking of tomorrow night's date instead of concentrating on the signal, a traffic citation may be your reward. If you fail to hear your instructor announce a quiz for the next class meeting because you were talking to a classmate, you cannot respond with study to a message you never received. Life is filled with communicative acts. If we are to function effectively, breakdowns must be kept to a minimum.

EXERCISES

1. Analyze the following cartoons as examples of communication, indicating the sender, message, receiver, and response. Where breakdowns in communication occur, indicate why.

"Hey! *This* isn't the best cup of coffee in town!"

Drawing by Lorenz; © 1971 The New Yorker Magazine, Inc.

Drawing by Chas. Addams; Copr. © 1931 The New Yorker Magazine, Inc.

"Phone for you, Al."

Drawing by Stevenson; © 1963 The New Yorker Magazine, Inc.

Drawing by W. Miller; © 1970 The New Yorker Magazine, Inc.

II. From your own experience, cite two examples of breakdowns, one involving speech, one involving writing.

1. Identify the causes of the breakdowns.
2. State what could have been done to improve the communication.

III. Study the following photographs and respond to the questions asked.

1. What is the message you receive from this photograph?
2. Suggest an appropriate caption.
3. How can we safeguard our environment from the effects of industrial pollution without endangering our economy? Cite an example of a specific industry in your response.
4. Investigate a company in or near your community alleged to be guilty of excessive pollution. Propose a solution that would safeguard the citizenry without driving the company out of business.

Reprinted with permission of the Milwaukee Journal.

Reprinted by permission of the photographer, Samuel Gansheroff.

1. Does the boy in the photograph have the same opportunities you had when you were his age? Discuss.
2. Suggest an appropriate caption.
3. Can we provide equality of opportunity for minority groups without infringing on the rights of the majority? Discuss.

Reprinted with permission of the photographer, Samuel Gansheroff.

1. How has our society handled the problems of its aged citizens? Discuss.
2. How have the chess players in the photograph adjusted to old age?
3. Suggest an appropriate caption.

Reprinted with permission of United Press International.

1. **What is your reaction to this photograph? Shock? Dismay? Indifference? Gladness? Explain.**
2. **Is such a marriage legal in your state? Should it be?**
3. **Discuss your feelings about the individuals involved: the two bridegrooms, their families, and the minister who officiated.**

SPEECHES AND COMPOSITIONS

I. DIRECTIONS: Develop a presentation, written (200–400 words) or oral (2–4 minutes), in which you: (1) introduce yourself to the audience; or (2) explain an area of interest, e.g., a sport, hobby, or pastime.

II. DIRECTIONS: Experience any two of the following sensitivity modules. Prepare a written report of one of the two experiences. Be prepared to relate the other to the class orally.

SENSITIVITY MODULES

1. Wear old clothes and sit in the waiting room of the Welfare Office. Listen, observe, read the announcements on the bulletin board, and talk to some of the other people there.

2. Attend a church service in a storefront church.

3. Go to an inner city elementary school and read a story to a child in kindergarten or first grade. The child must be held on your lap.

4. Go to magistrate's court and keep a list of the kinds of cases brought before the magistrate. Who are the "customers" being tried? How are they dealt with?

5. Sit in the waiting room of the maternity ward of a city hospital whose patients are mostly charity cases. Strike up a conversation with any other person in the waiting room.

6. Live for three days on the amount of money received by a typical welfare mother to feed a son or daughter close to your own age.

7. Read at least two issues, cover to cover, of a newspaper primarily aimed at a minority group.

8. Go to the community health center and take a place in line. Watch the attitude of the personnel who work there. Talk to some of the other patients coming for help.

9. Turn off the heat in your own house some night in January or February and spend the night in a cold house.

10. Read The Autobiography of Malcolm X, Manchild in the Promised Land, **or** some other book which tells what it is like to grow up black in America.

11. Attend a meeting of a civic group, such as the Human Relations Committee, the Welfare Rights Organization, or the Neighborhood Association.

12. Find a neighbor whose landlord has not given him heat, or has not repaired a roof leak or a toilet. Offer to help him get it fixed by calling City Hall and registering a complaint.